# NOTTINGHAMSHIRE

## A portrait in colour

DEREK FORSS & MIKE ASTILL

COUNTRYSIDE BOOKS

First published 2002
© Photographs, Derek Forss 2002
© Text, Mike Astill 2002

COUNTRYSIDE BOOKS
3 Catherine Road
Newbury, Berkshire

To view our complete range of books,
please visit us at
www.countrysidebooks.co.uk

ISBN 1 85306 759 8

Thanks go to the following for permission to take photographs:
Cropwell Bishop Creamery;
Nottinghamshire County Cricket Club Ltd, Trent Bridge;
National Ice Centre, Nottingham;
Broxtowe Borough Council, D.H. Lawrence Heritage Centre;
Hodsock Priory Gardens;
Ollerton Watermill & Teashop;
Blue Barn Farm, Langwith.

The photograph on page 4 shows Ollerton post office

Produced through MRM Associates Ltd., Reading
Printed in Italy

# Contents

# INTRODUCTION

Nottinghamshire is a county built on a wealth of history and legend, with an important industrial past … and a richly promising future.

Visitors from around the world continue to be drawn by the most written about and filmed of all medieval tales – the story of outlaw Robin Hood and his merry band – but they also find picturesque villages set in areas of lovely countryside, stately homes and country houses with wonderful gardens, restored canals, pride in the county's great literary figures, and the exciting city of Nottingham itself, 'the Queen of the Midlands'.

Within these pages you will find the essence of Nottinghamshire, its past, its present and its future, captured beautifully by the perceptive and evocative photographs of Derek Forss. You will explore Nottingham's history, visit Trent Bridge and the National Ice Centre, inspired by Torvill and Dean's international skating achievements, marvel at the intricate lace-making of the past, whirl on the Goose Fair's Big Wheel, shop under a magnificent glass dome, and stand awestruck in such contrasting buildings as the splendid Papplewick pumping station and Southwell Minster 'in a quietude of loveliness'.

Driving along the ancient Fosse Way – or travelling more sedately on one of the county's waterways, perhaps – you can go in search of D. H. Lawrence, his life and writings well documented in the University of Nottingham and the Birthplace Museum in the former mining community of Eastwood, or Lord Byron at Newstead Abbey, reflecting as you pass through the county on the generations who made Nottingham the top producing coal field in Europe and built up the framework knitting industry in harsh village frameshops.

I have lived in Nottinghamshire all my life and continue to be amazed at its variety. A county that can offer you maypole dancing and Robin Hood on the one hand and Olympic standard sports facilities and a futuristic tram system on the other is well worth exploring … enjoy it!

Mike Astill

# Historic Settlements along the Fosse Way

*Great roads the Romans built that men might meet,*
*And walls to keep strong men apart, secure.*
*Now centuries are gone, and in defeat,*
*The walls are fallen, but the roads endure.*
Ethelyn Miller Hartwich, *What Shall Endure?*

Draw a line with a ruler between Lincoln and Bath and you won't be too far off the route of the Fosse Way (*inset*), the A46. This Roman highway built in AD 47 carves through Nottinghamshire like a knife – with history spread richly all along its course.

Villages like Willoughby-on-the-Wolds (*opposite*) and Widmerpool have existed since Roman times, and nearby is Verometum, a Roman settlement where red flint road paving has been found. Further north, close to today's Bingham, the Roman settlement known as Margidunum existed until about AD 450.

Reminders of the far-reaching influence of the family who gave Willoughby village its name 700 years ago – they also built Nottingham's Wollaton Hall – are soon apparent when you visit the church of St Mary and All Saints. Effigies of Sir Hugh Willoughby, who died in 1445, and his wife, Margaret Freville, are prominent among the family's monuments. The figure of Sir Richard de Willoughby, an eminent lawyer who died in 1363, can be seen in his robes close to the north wall. During the Civil War the Battle of Willoughby Field was fought in 1648 and it is reported that villagers climbed the church steeple to watch the fighting.

The tiny hamlet of Owthorpe, with its picturesque church, St Margaret's, was once the home of John Hutchinson, one of the judges who signed the death warrant of Charles I.

Travelling towards Newark you come to the remarkable little village of East Stoke, which was not only the site of a Roman fort called Ad Pontem, but also the setting for one of England's bloodiest battles. Some 7,000 men died here in 1487, the last engagement in the War of the Roses. Over the years, farmers have turned up many remnants of the savage battle in areas since named 'Deadman's Field' and 'Red Gutter'. A spring at the heart of the carnage is said to sometimes run red, as if with the blood of soldiers.

# The Vale of Belvoir

*Many's the long night*
*I've dreamed of cheese*
Robert Louis Stevenson (1850-1894)

Shared with neighbouring Leicestershire, the Vale of Belvoir is one of Nottinghamshire's and England's loveliest areas of countryside. Largely unspoilt, it is a picturesque swathe of rolling countryside divided by the Grantham Canal and dotted with small traditional villages.

The unmissable feature of the Vale is, of course, Belvoir Castle, a magnificent stronghold dominating the landscape for many miles. Open to the public and regularly filmed as a true English castle, it is the home of the Duke and Duchess of Rutland and of the museum of the 17th/21st Lancers.

A rich agricultural area, the Vale of Belvoir is best known for its Stilton cheese. A popular myth is that the cheese originated from the village of Stilton, just south of Peterborough on the Great North Road, whereas, in fact, the name was adopted because the landlord of the Bell Inn there sold his sister-in-law's cheeses which were made near Melton Mowbray.

Today, award-winning Stilton cheeses continue to be made using traditional methods at dairies in Cropwell Bishop (*inset*), Colston Bassett and Long Clawson. Stilton cheese never has and never can be made at Stilton since trademark protection allows for the tasty after-dinner treat to be produced only in the neighbouring counties of Nottinghamshire, Leicestershire and Derbyshire.

The cheese-making process involves a maturing period over several weeks when the cheeses are turned regularly.

Stainless steel needles are pushed into the circumference to produce the growth of *Penicillium roqueforti* and the familiar bluish-coloured veins. Production reaches a peak of demand in time for the Christmas table but these days Stilton cheese sells all around the world.

# The Grantham Canal

*To travel hopefully is a better thing than to arrive*
Robert Louis Stevenson (1850-1894)

Nearly 70 years after the Grantham Canal was closed and abandoned, this 33 mile waterway which winds its way from Nottingham to Grantham through the beautiful Vale of Belvoir is coming back to life once again. But instead of barges hauling coal and supplies, it will be pleasure boats, anglers and leisure-time strollers making the most of the canalside walks and the lovely surrounding countryside.

First moves for a canal linking Nottingham and Grantham came in 1791 when a possible route was surveyed by William Jessop. By the end of that decade the waterway was in full flow with boats and barges carrying cargoes of coal, coke, farm produce and even passengers. But the arrival of railways and roads and much quicker and more efficient goods transport sounded the death knell of the canal. For more than 30 years after its closure in the mid 1930s it became derelict, locks fell into disrepair and many road bridges were flattened.

Canal enthusiasts formed a society in the 1960s to save the canal, although it was not until the 1980s that its potential was really seen. Teams of enthusiastic volunteers organised by the Grantham Canal Restoration Society set to work restoring sections of the canal – stretches at Denton, Hickling and Woolsthorpe Top Lock near Belvoir Castle being among the first to be reclaimed. Society members knew that their dream of seeing the full length of the canal in use again would be a reality when the county and the local councils agreed to give their support. And Lincolnshire County Council raised a low-level road bridge at Casthorpe, opening up 4½ miles.

At the Cotgrave section (*opposite*) new lock gates have been installed, canal paths opened up and a country park created alongside the canal where the colliery once operated.

# Bingham and Radcliffe-on-Trent

*The market is the best garden*

George Herbert (1593-1633)

The Buttercross (*opposite*), standing proudly in Bingham Market Place, forms a link between the villages of Bingham and Shelford since the monument, erected in 1861 on the site of a previous buttercross, is dedicated to John Hassall, who lived at Shelford Manor and was agent to the Earl of Chesterfield and the Earl of Carnarvon, Lord of the Manor of Bingham.

The Buttercross was the place where people from around the Vale of Belvoir would bring their home-made butter and cheese to sell at market. John Wesley preached

from there in 1770 and it was the scene of riots over butter prices in 1795. Discontinued in the late 19th century, the Thursday market was revived in 1975 and continues successfully today.

A few miles west of Bingham, high up on the cliffs of Radcliffe-on-Trent, a grieving father's love for his son led to the creation of one of the most beautiful parks in Nottinghamshire. Rockley Memorial Park (*inset*) was established in the late 1920s by Mr Lisle Rockley in memory of his son who was killed in the First World War. The lovely formal gardens enclosed by towering trees are a peaceful place for reflection just as they were more than 70 years ago.

Leading from the park is a splendid cliff walk overlooking the river valley from the top of the steep 'red cliffs'. In one direction it crosses the Malkin Hills towards Shelford while in the opposite direction it reaches Wharf Lane, once a busy calling point for boats, barges and ferries. Opposite the entrance and overlooking the village is St Mary's church which owes much of its present appearance to the Reverend John Cullen who instigated major rebuilding work in 1878. Close to the church against a recessed wall a whipping post and stocks stand as a reminder of brutal punishment of the past.

Reference is made to 'Radclyve' in the Domesday survey and there are reminders today, in the church and elsewhere, of families such as the d'Ayncourts and the Manvers, whose influence shaped the village.

# The River Trent

*The river glideth at his own sweet will*
William Wordsworth (1770-1850)

Once a great watery highway used as an important trade route, today the Trent offers more to leisure pursuits than to business and the economy. One of Britain's longest navigable rivers, it was an important route for the Romans, who called it Trisantona, and it was in the 8th century that it became known as Treonte.

This giant river dominates the landscape as it winds its way across Nottinghamshire, dictating the direction of those who need to cross it daily. The barges that used to transport goods, particularly coal, have been replaced by pleasure boats, narrowboats, rowing boats and canoes, and there are countless peaceful vistas, as at Stoke Bardolph (*opposite*).

The best-known port of call, famous the world over for its sporting links, is Nottingham's Trent Bridge, the first crossing at this point dating from AD 924. The famous county cricket ground nearby takes the name Trent Bridge while even closer is the City Ground home of Nottingham Forest, the all-conquering team of the 1970s which twice won the European Cup. On the opposite side of the river is the Football League's oldest club, Notts County.

South-west of Nottingham, a nature reserve and conservation area has been created from the worked-out gravel pits at Attenborough, where visitors can enjoy viewing the many species of birds, butterflies and wildlife.

At Newark the remains of the castle beside the river attract people from all over the world and the wharfside conversions are bringing a new lease of life to the town's riverside area. To the south-west at Fiskerton (*inset*) the gently curving Trent flows past the old wharf, still used by the river traffic, a picture of serene beauty and tranquillity.

# Holme Pierrepont

*The use of history is to give value to the present hour*
Ralph Emerson (1803–1882)

Holme Pierrepont has to be one of Nottinghamshire's smallest communities and yet it enjoys a world-wide reputation, the focus of sporting attention regularly turning on it when national and international rowing, canoeing and water skiing events are held at the National Water Sports Centre (*opposite*).

The Olympic-size rowing course and the water ski lake have been created out of the former gravel workings and water from the River Trent keeps canoeists and rafters hurtling down the white water slalom course.

Other visitors relax in the country park beside the river or pass a little further along the tiny country lane to reach historic Holme Pierrepont Hall (*inset*). Originally known as Holme, the Pierrepont was added in 1288 when heiress Annora de Manvers married Henry de Pierrepont. The Hall stands in a beautiful parkland setting, but the visitor first encounters the charming little church of St Edmond, which dates from the 13th century.

Built by Sir William Pierrepont, Holme Pierrepont is a fine example of an early Tudor dwelling and is one of the oldest surviving brick built houses. It was at its most impressive in the mid 1600s when it was the home of Robert Pierrepont, the 1st Earl of Kingston. But after 1680 the family preferred to live at Thoresby Hall in North Nottinghamshire.

Charles Meadows revived the estate when he inherited it and was created 1st Earl of Manvers. Extensive building work took place in the early 19th century. The elegant courtyard garden was designed in 1875 and today's owners are continuing to restore the Hall.

# The County's Cricket

*I tend to believe that cricket is the greatest
thing that God ever created on earth …*

Harold Pinter

As a cricket fan myself, I listened with interest as a team of expert commentators debated which English Test Match cricket ground they rated as the best. Well, it had to be Lord's, didn't it? But no, one by one the speakers cast their vote for Trent Bridge. The setting, the history, the new stands, the friendliness … it all confirmed what Notts supporters knew only too well.

Trent Bridge (*opposite*) has not only been the setting for numerous memorable Test Matches but also the home club of many legendary players, among them names such as Sobers, Hadlee, Randall and Clive Rice – the latter returning to manage the Nottinghamshire team after a career as one of the greatest international all-rounders.

Trent Bridge, which was founded in 1841, is the world's third oldest major cricket ground, after Lord's and Eden Gardens in Calcutta. It was founded way back in 1838 by William Clarke, who saw the potential of the ground and arranged for inter-county matches to be staged there.

Today, Trent Bridge is protecting its Test Match status by building some of the finest facilities in the country, including the giant £7.2 million Radcliffe Road stand, officially opened by Sir Gary Sobers in 1998.

Village cricket, in Nottinghamshire as elsewhere, is of course no less keenly contested and the timeless setting at Colston Bassett's tree-fringed ground in the Vale of Belvoir (*inset*) is typical of many in the county. Here, cricketers playing in the wonderfully named Washpit Lane are overlooked on one side by the hauntingly beautiful St Mary's church and on the other by Colston Basset Hall.

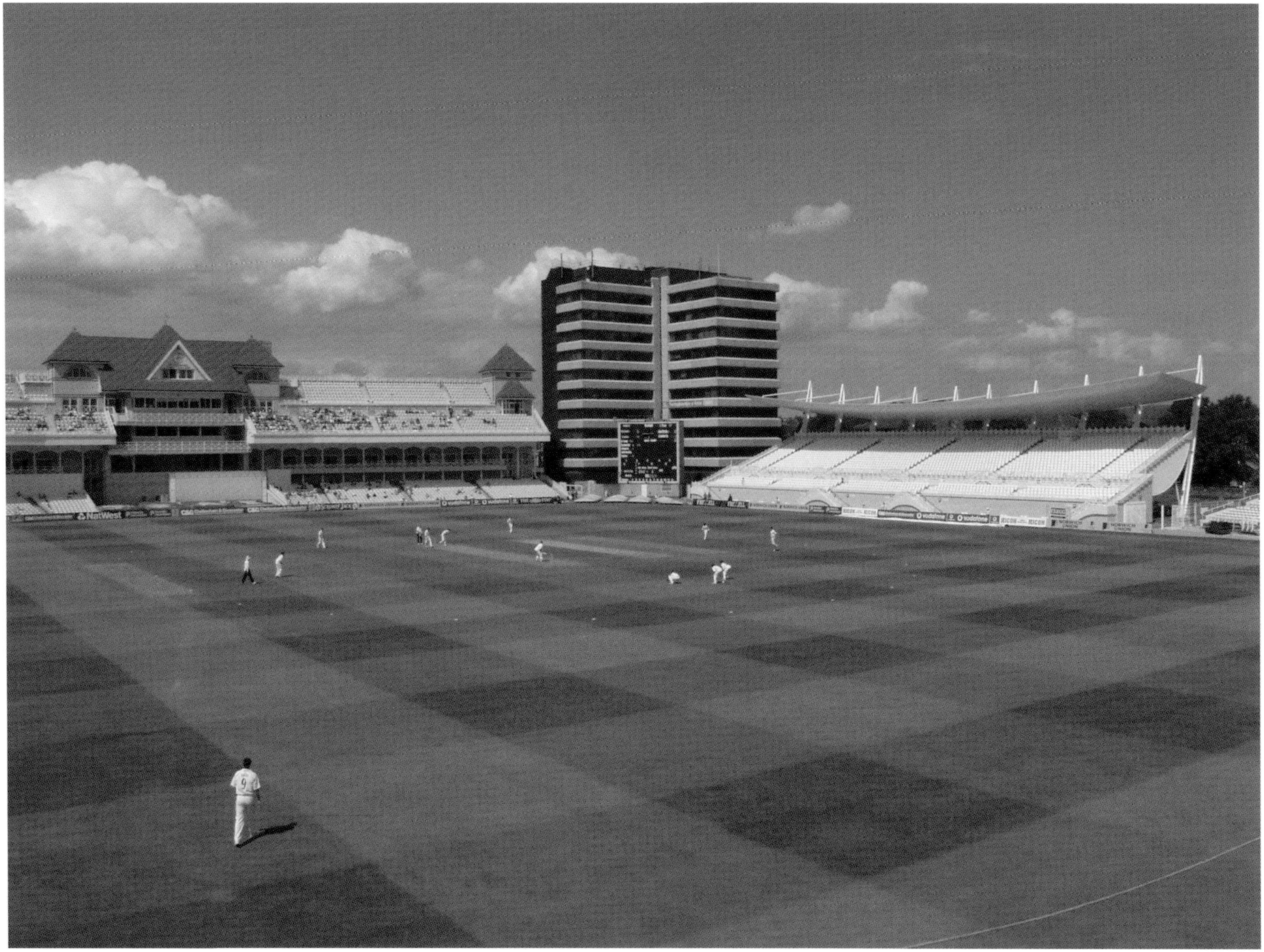

# Nottingham Canal and Green's Mill

*Take care … those things over there are not giants but windmills*
Miguel Cervantes (1547-1616), *Don Quixote*

It had its heyday in the 19th century as a busy cargo transport route and it reached its low point of dereliction in the 20th century, but the Nottingham Canal is back in fashion again. Old buildings along its course have been converted to luxury apartments, warehouse buildings are now popular restaurants, bars and clubs, and businesses are eager to relocate to a canalside setting (*opposite*).

Dating from 1792, the Nottingham Canal was extended in an age of canal building and linked five years later via the River Trent with the 33 miles of Grantham Canal. It opened up a network of routes by which barges could transport their cargoes. The canals thrived until the railways, and later the roads, caused their demise and only a new age of thinking is reviving the fortunes of these historic routes.

And how many cities can boast a working windmill within their boundaries? Green's Mill (*inset*) stands proudly at Belvoir Hill, Sneinton, its white sails turning in the wind, a monument to the brilliant 19th century mathematician and physicist George Green. It still produces flour for sale, while the adjoining Science Centre illustrates some of Green's scientific achievements.

Amazingly, before an ambitious restoration project by the City Council the mill had fallen into disrepair and was a barely recognisable fire-damaged shell.

Green's career was remarkable in view of his early life and background. He was born in Nottingham in 1794, the son of a baker, and received little formal education in childhood. He went into the family business, but with his interest in science growing he sold the mill at Sneinton after the death of his father in 1829 and went to Cambridge University where he studied from 1833 to 1840. He died in 1841 from influenza but left behind papers of original research, the importance of which were fully recognised in the 20th century.

# Nottingham's Landmark Buildings

*Castles are forests of stone.*

George Herbert (1593-1633)

Nottingham Castle is the stuff that legends are made of and its great history and links with the tale of Robin Hood continue to attract visitors worldwide.

As castles go Nottingham is unspectacular since it was destroyed in 1831 by Reform Bill rioters and restored as a museum 40 years later by the then Nottingham Corporation. But the gatehouse and much photographed bronze statue of Robin Hood (*opposite*) help to satisfy those who come in search of the legend.

Nottingham Castle dates from 1068 when William the Conqueror ordered its construction. On 22nd August 1642 Charles I raised his standard to begin the Civil War outside the walls at what is today Standard Hill. Soon afterwards the original castle was demolished and in 1674 the Duke of Newcastle bought the site and built a ducal palace.

The story of Robin Hood begins at the end of the 12th century. While Richard the Lionheart was still on the Crusades, his brother John seized Nottingham Castle and after becoming King in 1199 spent much time there. It was about then, we are told, that the outlaw Robin Hood gathered together his band to rob from the rich to give to the poor, to the annoyance of his arch enemy the Sheriff of Nottingham.

While the castle remains the city's most famous building, Nottingham Council House (*inset*) must rank as the best-known city landmark, with 'Meet you by the lions' a very familiar local saying.

The imposing Council House belies its age, appearing grand, even historic. However, work began as recently as 1927 on the building that would replace the former Exchange and there were many voices of protest at the consequent decision to move the Goose Fair and the regular market out of the square, from which point it became known as the Old Market Square.

Built of Portland stone taken from the same quarry used for St Paul's Cathedral, the terrace overlooking the square has eight huge columns above which are 21 figures. Overhead is the 10½ ton hour bell known as Little John, whose tones are renowned as the deepest in Britain.

# Ye Olde Trip to Jerusalem

*If die I must, let me die drinking in an inn*

Walter Map (1140-1210)

Not as famous as Robin Hood, but a Nottingham legend dating back to the days of the notorious outlaw is the Olde Trip to Jerusalem inn (*opposite*).

Sitting at the foot of Castle Rock, part carved from the sandstone rock and part building, the Olde Trip to Jerusalem is widely accepted as Britain's oldest pub. It carries the date 1189, the year of the accession to the throne of King Richard the Lionheart and, if the stories

are to be believed, would have existed in some form when the bad King John ruled the kingdom and Robin Hood and the evil Sheriff of Nottingham did battle.

The inn's unusual name is thought to refer to the journey of the Crusaders who met there before setting off on the long trip to the Middle East. Another theory is that it dates back to medieval times when Jewish money lenders were not allowed inside the castle walls. Instead they used the inn below as a meeting place and borrowers who travelled there were said to be taking a 'trip to Jerusalem'.

Either way, the myths and legends of this historic inn appeal to people from all around the world who mark their visit by leaving a note or coin of foreign currency.

Drinkers in the upstairs bar can look up high into a hole carved out of the rock and a back bar is known as the cave bar – for obvious reasons. Even the pub game is as old as the hills … a hoop hanging from a long rope attached to the ceiling invites drinkers to swing it over the ancient horn on the wall. Then there's the cursed galleon, a cobweb-covered ship with a reputation for bringing a horrible fate to anyone who moved it. A medium was hired to help put it into its present glass case after workmen refused to touch it.

Visitors can also take a tour of the caves under Nottingham Castle and see the famous Mortimer's Hole, an ancient passageway linking the top of Castle Rock and Brewhouse Yard (*inset*).

# Exchange Arcade

*Buying is a profound pleasure*
Simone de Beauvoir (1908-86)

Nottingham's reputation as the 'Queen of the Midlands' is earned for a variety of attributes, not least the excellence of its shopping. For many years it has ranked among the top six cities in Britain in retailing terms – not simply judged on numbers of shops, but for the quality and variety of goods on offer.

Many shoppers beat a trail between the huge Victoria and Broad Marsh shopping centres, but all around the city there are malls, walks, 'gates' and arcades to explore.

Right in the heart of these is Exchange Arcade, built within the imposing Nottingham Council House. Today, this very elegant shopping area has taken on the appearance of an exclusive fashion centre in its own right. Opened in 1929, it reflects many of the features of the neo-Baroque Council House building. A magnificent glass dome above the central walkway (*opposite*) is edged by four historical murals.

The arcade was originally, and for many years, occupied by Burtons, an exclusive food store, but in the early 1980s it underwent a major refurbishment and leading fashion names like Jeff Banks of Warehouse were among the first to see its potential. The longest established business in the arcade is Gauntley's the tobacconist, which first opened in 1880 on Long Row.

A short distance away on Victoria Street the magnificent Lewis & Grundy clock (*inset*) is back in its original 'home'. The clock is topped by two blacksmith figures which in its fully working days marked each quarter hour by hammering on the anvil. For many years it was over the entrance of Lewis & Grundy, wholesale ironmongers, whose store had entrances on both Pelham Street and Victoria Street. When the firm moved to Lenton they donated the clock to the city and it went to the Brewhouse Yard Museum, where it stayed for many years before being returned to its original position.

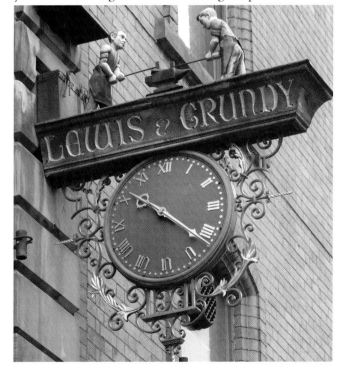

# The Goose Fair

*The thumping pistons of red-painted engines gave power to the Caterpillars and
Noah's Ark and distant screams came down at them from the tower of Helter Skelter*
Alan Sillitoe, *Saturday Night and Sunday Morning*

On the first weekend of October each year Nottingham experiences the phenomenon of the Goose Fair – a modern version of a fair dating back beyond medieval times. Showmen from all around Britain head for the city to transform (since the venue moved from the market square when the Council House was built in the 1920s) the huge Forest Recreation Ground from a quiet park and ride site into an extravaganza of whirling rides and deafening noise, over 100 rides and side shows, up to 500 stalls, all packed tightly on some 18 acres.

The night-time spectacle of acres of coloured lights is one that many visitors go just to see. But the fair is gone as quickly as it arrived. It is opened when the Lord Mayor rings a pair of silver bells and a proclamation is read. Traditionally it ran from Thursday to Saturday, but more recently it has been extended to a fourth day.

Arguably the world's oldest travelling fair, it is also famous for its mushy peas, Grantham gingerbreads, and its many traditional old rides – alongside the latest white knuckle, stomach churning machines.

The Goose Fair is believed to date back as far as 1284 when the Charter of King Edward I refers to a fair on the Feast of St Matthew being established in Nottingham. It is thought to take its name from the time when hundreds of geese were driven from Lincolnshire and Norfolk to be sold in Nottingham. There are clear records of the fair dating back to 1541 when in the Chamberlain's account in the Nottingham Borough records there is reference to an allowance of 1s 10d for 22 stalls taken by the city's two Sheriffs on Goose Fair Day.

# The National Ice Centre

*Many congratulations on your superb performance, which I watched with great pleasure and which brought you such a well-deserved gold medal.*
Queen Elizabeth on Jayne Torvill and Christopher Dean's perfect
12 sixes to win gold in the 1984 Sarajevo Winter Olympics

When in 1995 it was decided to build a National Ice Centre, Nottingham's long-lasting love affair with ice skating and unparalleled success made the city's Lottery Fund bid another winner.

The original ice stadium where Jayne Torvill and Christopher Dean learned their ice dance routines was bulldozed to the ground and a new £40 million National Ice Centre with two Olympic-sized ice pads was built on the site. It opened in April 2000.

The first built and largest stadium is called the Arena since along with the capability to host international skating events, the rink can be covered to form a concert hall holding audiences of up to 10,000 and can convert to a variety of uses such as for soccer tournaments and show jumping. It is also the home of the Panthers ice hockey team. The second ice pad is intended mainly for public skating.

Torvill and Dean, who were both involved in the development of the new centre and are members of its charitable trust, played a big part in securing the £22.5 million grant from the Lottery Sports Fund.

Their success in the 1980s elevated ice dance to new levels and really put Nottingham and British ice skating on the map. As British, European and World champions they went to the 1984 Winter Olympics in Sarajevo, Yugoslavia and set the sporting world alight with their 'Bolero' routine, scoring a row of 12 perfect sixes from the judges.

It was what the British public wanted to see as record numbers tuned in to watch the now legendary performance. There cannot be many sports performers to have received personal congratulations from the Queen, who was one of the many avid viewers. The couple are among a small and select number to have been granted the Freedom of the City of Nottingham.

# Nottingham Lace

*Clothes introduced sewing, a kind of work which you may call endless; a woman's dress, at least, is never done*

H.D. Thoreau (1817–1862)

In the boom years of the mid 19th century highly fashionable Nottingham lace was in such demand that intensive hand production was overtaken by machines and by 1865 there were well over 100 factories producing lace in a vast range of patterns.

The legacy of the once great lace industry is Nottingham's famous Lace Market area, though the visitor may be surprised to find no lace being produced there today. Instead the quarter square mile area of towering buildings, once a bustling hive of lace factories and warehouses, has found a new 'city living' use as apartments, restaurants, cafés and bars, combined with offices, shops and colleges.

The first forms of lace production were bobbin lace and needle lace but by 1760 lace was being made on framework knitting machines invented about 175 years earlier by the Reverend William Lee of Calverton. In 1808 the machine lace industry was really born when John Heathcote invented a hand operated lace-making machine. Five years later John Leavers produced a machine capable of making 18 inch wide plain net and subsequent developments brought machines that could produce fabric of complex design at a fraction of the handmade prices. Steam power and patterning attachments invented by Joseph Marie Jacquard moved the industry even further forward.

Lace enjoyed a boom between the 1880s and the First World War. Ornate Nottingham lace was used extensively on ladies' clothing and styles became very elaborate. Lace was also used widely in the home.

Today, lace continues to be made in Nottingham by a few large companies targeting specific high street and export markets, and as a fashion item it is most popular for lingerie. The Museum of Nottingham Lace (*opposite*) in High Pavement tells the story of the city's lace industry, with demonstrations and fascinating displays. The Lace Centre, in a pretty 15th century house in Castle Road, has lace hanging from every beam (*inset*), much of it for sale.

# The University of Nottingham

*O this learning, what a thing it is!*
William Shakespeare, *The Taming of the Shrew*

The University of Nottingham, with its magnificent buildings, gardens (*inset*), boating lake and croquet lawns, is there to be used and enjoyed by the people of Nottingham and not just by the 23,000-plus students who come to Nottingham for their education.

Unlike some universities that are tightly packed into cities, Nottingham's University Park campus sprawls over 330 acres between Beeston, Wollaton, Lenton and Dunkirk.

In the same way that Sir Jesse Boot made the Boots Company one of Britain's biggest and most successful companies, so his influence on the university has been profound. The original University College in Nottingham city centre became outgrown by the increasing number of students and after the First World War Jesse Boot provided money and the site for the university to expand.

It was established in 1948 with the granting of a Royal Charter and more than 50 years later the university has seen major developments and growth. These include the creation of England's first post-war Medical School which is directly linked with the Queen's Medical Centre. An award-winning library was followed by the construction of a £5 million Arts Centre on the site of the former Highfields Lido.

The university has four campuses and many other locations in an around the city – and even as far away as Kuala Lumpur. In 1999 the Queen opened Jubilee Campus, a £50 million development over 30 acres with state-of-the-art academic and residential buildings.

A resources centre is dedicated to one of the university's most famous sons, D.H. Lawrence. This houses the complete works of the Eastwood-born novelist, playwright and poet, and includes many original manuscripts.

# Wollaton Hall and Park

*He builded better than he knew,*
*The conscious stone to beauty grew*

Ralph Emerson (1803–1882)

Wollaton Hall and Park must be one of the most wonderful examples of a mansion house and estate that are within a city's boundaries and entirely open for public use. There are more than 500 acres of parkland roamed by the famous herd of deer, a lake, golf course and within the house and courtyard are a Natural History Museum and Nottingham's Industrial Museum.

The Hall was the home of the Willoughby family for more than 300 years. It was built between 1580 and 1588

by Sir Francis Willoughby, whose family included the explorer Sir Hugh Willoughby who died on a 16th century expedition to the Arctic, and Francis Willoughby the famous naturalist (1635–72) whose natural history collections are preserved at Wollaton.

The Hall, designed by architect Robert Smythson, is a Grade I listed building and an outstanding example of Renaissance architecture. It is said that the Ancaster stone from which it is built was brought by packhorses from Lincolnshire quarries and on their return journey the horses carried coal from Wollaton pits.

The very elaborate, elegant building has more than 200 statues and the great central hall rises over 50 feet. Above it is the Prospect Room from which there are magnificent views all around the estate.

Adjacent to the Hall is the Stable Block, where today the city's Industrial Museum is housed and visitors should not miss the Camellia House, another listed structure, which is still in use as a hot house, and the caves including the 'Admiral's Bath'.

The Park, which is open to the public and where city events and shows are held, contains many fine trees and an avenue of limes planted by the Lords Middleton in the latter part of the 18th century. The Hall and Park were bought by the Corporation of Nottingham in 1925 for £200,000 … a pretty sound investment!

# Ruddington

*Man goes forth to his work, and to his labour until the evening*
Psalm 104, verse 23

Today, a busy south Nottinghamshire village popular as a place to live while commuting to work in Nottingham, Ruddington was once a hive of industry in its own right, a mini centre of thriving 19th century framework knitting. But unlike so many places where history has been forgotten, Ruddington's long and distinguished past has been faithfully captured in two village museums, thanks to the work of local people.

Ruddington Framework Knitters' Museum, housed in restored workshops, cottages and frameshops (*inset*), brings visitors the complete experience of the harsh, labour-intensive conditions involved in working the stocking frame machines.

Invented just a few miles away in Calverton by the Reverend William Lee in 1589, the stocking frame was to launch an extensive framework knitting industry with many thousands employed in Nottingham and around the county – Ruddington having a particularly large community of framework knitters. By the mid 19th century some two-thirds of the village's working population were involved in the hosiery business. Samuel Parker, and later his son William Parker, established one set of workshops employing 150 people including women and children.

Nowadays, the hand framer and circular sock machines are put into daily use in the working museum (*opposite*).

A short distance away on Church Street, Ruddington Village Museum, housed in a former school, perfectly complements the Framework Knitters' Museum by depicting other village achievements in the early years of the 20th century when framework knitting began to decline. There are several reconstructed shops, an Edwardian fish and chip shop, a pharmacist, a cobbler's, an ironmonger's and a toy shop. There is also an Edwardian schoolroom and collection of farm implements.

# Scarrington

*Under the spreading chestnut tree*
*The village smithy stands*
Henry Wadsworth Longfellow (1807-1882), *The Village Blacksmith*

There are parts of Nottinghamshire that are still essentially undevel ped rural areas. Little known to the casual passer-by, because they are away from main roads, their appearance has changed little in the last 300 years. One such area is north of Bingham, stretching eastwards from the A46 to the Leicestershire border. There is little industry in this part of the county. It is here that Scarrington, one of a score of small villages, can be found. Two adjacent structures are the pride of Scarrington, and an illustrated information board details them. The well-restored circular pound or pinfold is one of a number of such little buildings in the county, which were a necessity in medieval times when fields were open. A village official, the pinder, had the job of rounding up stray animals and securing them in the pinfold until they were claimed. The owner had to pay a fine for the release, one penny in the 18th century for a horse or cow, and fourpence for a sow and pigs.

The other structure described on the board is unique. This is a pile of horseshoes standing 17 feet high and 19 feet 6 inches in circumference (*inset*), just outside the former village smithy. There are about 50,000 horseshoes, weighing about 10 tons, and they are interlocked without any other support. The pile was built up from June 1945 to April 1965 by George Flinders, a blacksmith at the forge for 51 years.

# D.H. Lawrence

*I am a man, and alive … For this reason I am a novelist. And being a novelist, I
consider myself superior to the saint, the scientist, the philosopher, and the poet*
D.H. Lawrence, *Why the Novel Matters*

Best known even today for the controversy that surrounded his novels, David Herbert Lawrence is one of Nottinghamshire's most famous sons, a brilliant and sensitive writer of poems, plays and novels. His upbringing in a Nottinghamshire mining community in Victorian Britain was the backdrop for some of his finest works, even though in later years Lawrence chose to live abroad for much of the time.

'DH' Lawrence, as he has come to be famously known, was born in Eastwood in 1885, a very traditional coal mining area in the Erewash Valley. His father, Arthur, worked at nearby Brinsley Colliery.

Young David Lawrence was educated at Nottingham High School and University College, Nottingham, and after teaching in Croydon and surviving serious illness, he returned to Nottingham, met Frieda Weekley, the wife of a Nottingham college professor, and eloped to Germany and Italy with her.

Lawrence's early work included *Love Poems and Others* (1913) and *Sons and Lovers* in the same year. During the First World War he wrote *The Rainbow*, the first of his books to be subjected to censorship and suppression … the other being his best-known book *Lady Chatterley's Lover*, which was the subject of a landmark indecency trial in the 1960s. Lawrence also produced many plays including *A Collier's Friday Night*, *The Widowing of Mrs Holroyd* and *Touch and Go*.

For much of the last ten years of his life Lawrence lived abroad and travelled extensively in Europe, Mexico and Australia. He died in France in 1930.

The tiny terraced house in Victoria Street, Eastwood where Lawrence was born is now a Birthplace Museum recreated in the style in which he and his family would have lived (*opposite and inset*). Durban House Heritage Centre nearby tells the story of Lawrence's life and times.

# Grand Pumping Stations

*Monuments last much longer than words.*
*Civilizations are remembered by buildings.*
*There's nothing more important than architecture.*

Philip Johnson (US architect)

If a water pumping station were built today I am sure it would be functional, computer controlled and tucked away in an inconspicuous building. However, the pumping stations built in Victorian times in Nottinghamshire stand as great Gothic cathedral-like structures, testimony to an age of elaborate construction.

Papplewick pumping station built between 1882 and 1884, remains the most unaltered of the few splendid examples in the county. Commissioned to pump water to supply Nottingham's rapidly increasing population, no expense was spared in creating a magnificent building to house two massive steam-driven beam engines (*inset*) which, when in full steam, are a breathtaking sight. The building was designed by city engineer Marriott Ogle

Tarbotton, who created a monument even more remarkable than his name!

Papplewick pumping station remains in full working order with regular 'steaming days' for the public who stand in awe, watching the mighty movement of huge flywheels 20 feet in diameter and weighing 24 tons.

The extensively ornamented building has eight stained glass windows depicting water plants, giant columns decorated with bronze friezes of birds, fishes, bullrushes and waterfalls, and incorporates six hand-fired Lancashire boilers. Standing alongside beautiful gardens and a man-made lake, the station is listed as one of the top ten industrial monuments in Europe.

Bestwood pumping station, which also supplied Nottingham with its water, was stripped of its machinery once out of commission, but the derelict building has since been faithfully restored and now has a new lease of life as a restaurant and health spa.

Boughton pumping station (*opposite*) in the north of the county has also found a new beginning after being transformed from near dereliction to become an award-winning visitor centre.

The giant pump engine from the former Basford waterworks takes pride of place in the Industrial Museum at Nottingham's Wollaton Hall and can regularly be seen in full steam.

# Newstead Abbey

*But words are things, and a small drop of ink,*
*Falling like dew upon a thought, produces*
*That which makes thousands, perhaps millions, think*
Lord Byron (1788-1824), *Don Juan*

Newstead Abbey, with its haunting Priory church front, beautiful lake and gardens, historic past and association with the poet Lord Byron, is one of Nottingham's great treasures.

Founded in 1170 by Henry II, as the Priory of Saint Mary at Newstead, it was for 400 years an active religious community run by the Regular Canons of the Order of St Augustine. In 1539 the Priory was dissolved by Henry VIII during the Reformation and the following year, together with Papplewick Manor and 750 acres, it was bought by Sir John Byron of Colwick for £810 from the King.

The 5th Lord Byron, known as 'the wicked Lord', was tried in 1765 for the murder of his neighbour in a drunken duel, but escaped the charge. He later died in debt in the dilapidated Newstead building.

The title and Newstead passed to George Gordon Byron (1788-1824), who was to become one of Britain's greatest poets. Today, original manuscripts, letters and first editions by Lord Byron are on view in the Byron museum and visitors to the Abbey can see many of the poet's belongings, including a superb gilt four-poster bed. There is a fine collection of English and Continental furniture, a collection of Crimean War relics, 14th and 15th century manuscripts and relics of the medieval building.

In 1817, living in Italy and with mounting debts, Byron sold the Abbey to Colonel Thomas Wildman, an old school friend, who began extensive restorations. When Colonel Wildman died in 1859, the Abbey was bought by William Webb, an African explorer and friend of Dr Livingstone.

Improvements to the building continued and after Webb died in 1899 Newstead passed to successive generations of his family until his grandson sold it to Nottingham businessman Sir Julien Cahn who, in 1931, presented it to the present owners, the City of Nottingham.

# Newark-on-Trent

*We will probably be judged not by the monuments we build, but by the ones we destroy*

Anon

Newark, situated alongside the River Trent and at the crossroads of the Roman Fosse Way and the Great North Road, has long been of strategic importance. The beautiful church of St Mary Magdalene, with its 240 ft spire, soars above the market town, but it is Newark

Castle (*opposite*) that dominates the history of the area.

Built in 1129 by the Bishop of Lincoln, the castle played an important role in the Civil War which began in 1642 when Charles I raised the royal standard in Nottingham. A garrison was established at Newark to secure a vital crossing over the river for munitions and, as a result, the Royalist town had to withstand sieges in 1643, 1644, and in 1646. But in May 1646, after the garrison had finally surrendered, Oliver Cromwell ordered the townspeople to demolish the castle.

Thankfully they did not destroy it completely and today the remains of the front wall, part of the tower and gatehouse are a big attraction for visitors to the historic town.

To many, St Mary Magdalene is regarded as one of the largest and finest parish churches in the country; the medieval Market Place (*inset*) is well known too and regular markets continue to be held there.

Newark is a mix of the historic and the unobtrusively modern and there are courts and alleyways full of surprises. Among the outstanding buildings is the Old White Hart, which is 700 years old and a fine example of Early English domestic architecture. Near to Newark Castle is the Ossington Coffee Palace, a hugely imposing building built in 1881 as a temperance establishment.

William Gladstone, who was MP for Newark between 1832 and 1846, is one of the many famous names associated with the town.

# Southwell

*We can only pray that when an angel beckons us it will be to some such heaven as Southwell*

Arthur Mee (1875–1943)

Author and historian Arthur Mee asked the question: 'Is there in England a greater surprise than the least known cathedral of Southwell Minster?' And he describes it as having 'dignity and beauty unsurpassed. The rushing tide of life has passed it by and left it standing in a quietude of loveliness, like some dream of time gone by.'

The present Norman church with its distinctive pointed twin towers (*inset*) was built between 1108 and 1150. It replaced an earlier Saxon church on the site which dated from AD 956. In 1884 when the new diocese of Southwell was formed, the town's magnificent church of St Mary the Virgin became its cathedral. The diocese covered Nottinghamshire and Derbyshire until Derby Cathedral was consecrated in 1927, and Southwell remains the smallest cathedral 'city' in England.

The market town of Southwell has many old and interesting buildings – too many to list in this brief chapter – but one of the most famous is the Saracen's Head, a former coaching inn where many royal personages have stayed, most famously King Charles I on his last night of freedom in 1646.

Established in the 12th century, the inn was originally known as the King's Arms, but was renamed the Saracen's Head Hotel in 1651 as an insult to the monarchy since King Charles was beheaded for high treason in London in 1649, a Saracen's sword from the time of the Holy Wars being used for the execution. An Elizabethan wall painting dating from 1590 was discovered during refurbishment work in 1986 and has been carefully restored and preserved.

There are reminders around the town that Southwell is the home of the Bramley apple. The first tree was grown from pips planted in a garden by a young girl, Mary Ann Brailsford, in 1809.

# Mansfield

*The mill goes toiling slowly round*
*With steady and solemn creak*
Eugene Field (1850-1895)

Mansfield, a royal manor in Norman times, has had a long history of importance because of its position on the western edge of Sherwood Forest. It was also a significant market town, being one of the two largest centres of population after Nottingham.

The coming of the railways altered the town's appearance and helped to increase its trade, particularly for the products of quarrying in the neighbourhood. The very good Mansfield stone was often used for building churches; sand, too, was in great demand.

In 1832 *White's Directory of Nottinghamshire* described Mansfield thus: 'from the gloomy colour of the stone of which the houses are built, the town has generally a sombre aspect and until a few years ago was proverbially dirty and badly paved ...' It went on to say, however, that from 1823 it had been well paved and lighted with gas and had risen to be a clean and commodious town.

Mansfield continued to grow during the 19th century, helped by the changes in textile manufacturing, from the use of handlooms to steam-powered mills. The opening of a number of collieries in the area provided employment for many men, which no doubt was responsible for the establishment of the large (eponymous) brewery. The importance of all this growth was emphasised in 1891 when the town received a charter for incorporation as a municipal borough.

The last hundred years have not been kind to Mansfield, since its reliance on basic industries, railways and coal has led to a reduction in employment opportunities. But the opening of the Robin Hood railway line from Nottingham to Worksop has enabled Mansfield's handsome Italianate station to be restored and a journey northwards gives a bird's eye view of the town as one crosses the spectacular high-arched bridge above the streets.

# Nottinghamshire's Black Gold

*We may well call it black diamonds,*
*Every basket is power and civilisation,*
*For coal is a portable climate.*

Ralph Emerson (1803–1882)

Coal mining is as much a part of Nottinghamshire as Robin Hood and lace. In its heyday in the 1960s and 70s more than 30 mines around the county, producing fuel mainly for British industry, made Nottingham the top producing coal field in Europe.

Miners from worked-out pits in the North-East and Scotland poured into Nottinghamshire on the promise of jobs for life extracting the rich black gold. But by the end of the century most of the pits had gone, leaving mining communities without mines and miners having to learn new skills.

At the height of coal production in Nottinghamshire some 40,000 men produced over 25 million tons of coal a year with more than half the collieries delivering a million tons, most of which went to a grid of coal-fired power stations for the electricity generating industry. Moreover the county led the way not only in production, but in advances in mechanised coal extraction.

Today, only half a dozen pits continue to operate, all in private hands, the coal industry's bubble having burst under pressure from other fuel sources such as oil and natural gas. And the industry went through a damaging period of strikes in the early 1980s when attempts were made to close collieries and streamline the industry, as a result of which Nottinghamshire's miners broke away from the National Union of Mineworkers to form their own body, the Union of Democratic Mineworkers. Many of the once bustling pit sites have been put to alternative uses as industrial and business parks and country parks for leisure use.

At Clipstone colliery (*opposite*) a country park, Vicar Water, has been created and a huge sculpture of a golden hand (*inset*) rises from the ground, symbolising the miners' belief that all life and wealth is taken from, and grows out of, the earth.

# Creswell Crags

*Death alone discloses how insignificant are the puny bodies of men*

Juvenal, *Satires*

What a remarkable county Nottinghamshire is! Not only do we have the Robin Hood legend and attractions such as Sherwood Forest, Nottingham Castle and Newstead Abbey bringing visitors from all around the world, but in the far north of the county is one of the world's most important Stone Age sites.

Creswell Crags, a collection of caves in a limestone gorge, was once home to Ice Age hunters, some 45,000 years ago. Archaeologists have unearthed evidence of both Neanderthal and modern hunters using the caves in the safety of the hidden valley for shelter. Tools made from stone, flint and bone have been found as well as the remains of humans, mammoths, reindeer and wild horses. Creswell Crags is the most northerly place in the world where Neanderthal remains have been found … and it also provides the earliest evidence of cave engravings in Britain.

The main caves, named Robin Hood's Cave, Grundy's Parlour, Churchhole and Pin Hole, can all be visited by the public on a special tourist trail. It is believed that they were used as temporary summer shelter by Neanderthals as they followed deer herds north. Sadly, Victorian archaeologists removed important finds from the site without documenting their work and many significant archaeological 'treasures' have been lost for ever.

Legend has it that Robin Hood took refuge in the Creswell Crags caves, but there is no evidence to support this. Today, Creswell Crags is carefully managed, with a museum and Education Centre offering special events, displays and presentations. Great efforts are being made to achieve World Heritage status for the site.

# Thoresby Hall

*The principle of Gothic architecture is infinity made imaginable*
Samuel Taylor Coleridge (1772-1834), *Table Talk*

Deep in the heartland of Sherwood Forest, one of Nottinghamshire's most famous houses, Thoresby Hall, stands resplendent.

The famous Grade I listed Victorian mansion, built in the Gothic style has been faithfully restored today after having fallen into disrepair and even being placed on English Heritage's 'at risk' register.

The present building dates from 1865 with two earlier grand houses having stood on the site. It was originally designed for the 3rd Earl Manvers, and architect Anthony Salvin incorporated Gothic features as a Victorian reaction to the traditional country house. Salvin's other local mansion, Harlaxton Manor, is an even more extravagant example of the Gothic style.

Inside, Thoresby's diverse state rooms reflect the different tastes of the 3rd Earl and his French wife. Deciding to decorate a room each, her Blue Room is a vision of the French Second Empire with a vibrant blue decoration. The adjoining library, by contrast, has a deeply Gothic feel with a spectacular wooden fireplace incorporating hand carved scenes of Sherwood Forest and beautifully fashioned figures of Robin Hood and Little John.

The Hall, which more recently was the regional headquarters of the former National Coal Board, contains two curious follies in its grounds. One is a large stone coffin-like structure erected in memory of Prime Minister Spencer Perceval who, in 1812, was shot and killed in the House of Commons by bankrupt Liverpool broker John Bellingham, who was later hanged.

The other folly, known as Nelson's Pyramid, a strange-looking domed room and stone porch, has details of naval battles inscribed on the walls. Both the 1st Earl Manvers and his son, the 2nd Earl, had served in the Royal Navy as captains.

# Sherwood Forest and the Major Oak

*Woodman, spare that tree!*
*Touch not a single bough!*
*In youth it sheltered me,*
*And I'll protect it now*

G.P. Morris (1802-1864)

According to legend – and legends are much more enduring than scientific fact – Sherwood Forest and its heathland (*inset*) was once roamed by the outlaw Robin Hood and his band of merry men. Perhaps the most tangible part of the Sherwood story is the Major Oak where Robin and other members of his company are said to have hidden from their enemies inside the hollow trunk.

I well remember as a boy playing around the mighty tree (*opposite*) and hiding inside it. Unfortunately, my feet and those of thousands of visitors compacted the soil around the famous oak and almost killed it. In the mid 1970s when the new Visitor Centre was built at Edwinstowe, the County Council had the good sense to fence off the tree and begin a conservation exercise to conserve it.

Estimated to weigh some 23 tons, the Major Oak is reckoned to be between 800 and 1,000 years old. Around 1908, metal chains and straps were used to support some brances across its 92 foot spread. Today, wooden supports prop up the huge branches of Britain's most famous and most visited tree.

It is named after Major Haymen Rooke, a local historian who wrote a book about the remarkable oaks of Sherwood Forest. These days, even greater efforts are being made to ensure the continuance of the Major Oak … saplings are grown from the tree's acorns and clones of the tree are provided each year.

Sherwood Forest once covered a third of Nottinghamshire and was a royal hunting preserve for English kings. But the royal hold over Sherwood ended after the fall of Charles I and large parts of the forest became privately owned. By Victorian times much of North Nottinghamshire had been divided into The Dukeries – estates owned by the Dukes of Portland, Newcastle, Leeds, Norfolk and Kingston.

# Welbeck and Rufford Abbeys

*I envy them, those monks of old,*
*Their books they read, and their beads they told*
G.P.R. James (1799-1860), *The Monks of Old*

In the 12th century the sparsely populated northern half of Nottinghamshire was an ideal place for men seeking solitude to establish religious houses. One of these was Thomas of Cuckney who founded a Premonstratensian monastery at Welbeck in Sherwood Forest. The monks would have cleared a large area for cultivation to produce food.

After the Dissolution, Welbeck was sold and was one of the estates incorporated into the area that became known as The Dukeries. Its 3,000 acres, which include extensive woodland and a lake, lie to the south of Worksop and extend westwards almost to the Derbyshire border. Some parts of the present building on the site were among the original monastic buildings but the remainder is a result of subsequent additions and remodelling, in particular after a fire in 1902. Today, part of Welbeck Abbey (*opposite*) is occupied as an Army college, while the rest is privately owned.

To the south-east, Rufford Abbey, the only Cistercian house in the county, was founded in 1146 by Gilbert Gant. Four hundred years later it was sold to the Saville family who had extensive properties in Yorkshire, and the monastic buildings fell into disrepair, although a new mansion was eventually built on to the remains. After a further four hundred years, when economics and changing social conditions were causing the demise of many aristocratic estates, Rufford was purchased by

Nottinghamshire County Council. Extensive work has been carried out to create the Country Park, open all year round for everyone to enjoy, with nature trails, a children's playground and, at the north end, a former mill which is now an exhibition centre.

Visit Rufford yourself and discover the ice-house, the racehorses' graves and the sculpture park, not to mention the impressive restoration work on the medieval Abbey (*inset*).

# Clumber Park

*When we build, let us think that we build for ever*

John Ruskin (1819-1900)

Once the home of the Dukes of Newcastle, Clumber Park at the heart of Sherwood Forest is today controlled by the National Trust, welcoming thousands of visitors each year. Remnants like the extensive kitchen garden, the Gothic Revival chapel (*opposite*), the impressive gated entrances, bridge and lake are reminders of times when Clumber House was at the centre of a vast self-sufficient estate.

The original Clumber House was built in 1768 for the 2nd Duke of Newcastle, but much of it was destroyed by fire in 1879. Subsequently rebuilt with an even more

palatial interior, in 1912 fire struck again and further rebuilding was needed.

Clumber's kitchen garden dates back to 1772 and in the late 1890s the 7th Duke renovated the garden and had the 450 yard long range of glasshouses built. In the early 1900s the gardens were in their heyday with 29 gardeners employed to help keep the house well supplied. The National Trust is now restoring the famous kitchen garden, reintroducing many old vegetables from Edwardian days and offering 'Taste Tests' to visitors to compare the taste of today's vegetables with those from a previous age.

The 87 acre lake was created in the 1770s and the Dukes of Newcastle enjoyed sailing boats and had a number of scale model vessels made. One, known as the *Lincoln,* sank after a fire and still remains at the bottom of the lake.

The estate went into decline after the death of the 7th Duke in 1928 and ten years later the house was demolished and the fixtures and fittings were sold. The National Trust purchased the property in 1946 as part of its Golden Jubilee celebrations and maintain the grounds and the chapel.

The Avenue of Limes (*inset*) is one of the most distinctive features of Clumber Park. Planted in 1838 by the 4th Duke, it is the longest such avenue in Europe, with 1,296 trees along a 3 mile stretch of road between Apleyhead Lodge and Carburton Lodge.

# East Retford

*The use of travelling is to regulate imagination by reality, and instead of thinking how
things may be, to see them as they are*

Samuel Johnson (1709-1784)

Today, East Retford cannot be found on road maps. For centuries East and West Retford, although separated only by the River Idle, were legally different. East Retford had since the 13th century been a municipal borough while West Retford was only a parish. Now they coexist, without any visible difference, as Retford.

On the old Great North Road, with the Idle providing communication between Worksop and the River Trent, this market town, surrounded by villages, received an additional bonus in the 18th century when the Chesterfield Canal came through it. Communications had also been helped by the turnpiking of four roads leading to East Retford.

In the 19th century the railway improved travel still further, and now Retford has two stations, one serving the east-west line between Sheffield and Lincoln, and the other the high-speed line from London to Edinburgh.

To absorb its character, there are two ways to visit Retford. On a sunny market day morning, the centre with its variety of stalls presents an animated scene. The 20th century increase in motor vehicles has mainly been contained on the perimeter of the town; visitors park a little away from the centre whilst a busy bus station accommodates shoppers from the villages.

The late afternoon or early evening shows Retford in a quieter mood. One can then appreciate the size and spaciousness of the market place, at the end of which is the Victorian Town Hall and the ancient Broad Stone. Nearby are St Swithun's church and Sloswicke's Hospital, a delightful building founded in 1657. Or you could do worse than linger awhile in King's Park (*inset*) where the River Idle runs its merry course.

Cannon Square is aptly named in recognition of the unmissable Russian cannon that stands there (*opposite*). Captured in 1855 at the Battle of Sebastapol, it was brought to Retford four years later through the efforts of local author John Shadrack Piercy as a memorial to the Crimean War, in which his son fought.

# Gringley and West Stockwith

*There is nothing – absolutely nothing – half so much worth*
*doing as simply messing about in boats.*
Kenneth Grahame (1859-1932), *The Wind in the Willows*

The countryside around the lovely North Nottinghamshire village of Gringley-on-the-Hill (*opposite*) is made all the more attractive for the dedication of those canal preservation volunteers determined not to allow this section of the Chesterfield Canal, with its distinctive locks, tunnels and features, to be lost.

This is a popular destination for narrowboat and pleasure boat enthusiasts wanting to enjoy some of the most picturesque and traditionally unchanged parts of the county. One of the features not to be missed by the new generation of canal travellers is the Drakeholes tunnel.

Renowned canal builder James Brindley produced his plans for a canal from Chesterfield to Worksop in 1769. The subsequent line of the canal northwards from East Retford could have followed the River Idle, but while the river went on a long detour before reaching West Stockwith and the River Trent, avoiding high ground at Everton, Brindley decided on a more direct course through the hill.

The Drakeholes tunnel was completed in 1772, although Brindley died before the five months of work was finished. The tunnel was 154 yards long and driven through sandstone so hard that the customary brick lining was not needed. There was no towpath, so the horses pulling the barges had to be led over the hill to the other side. Normally the boatmen would move the boat through the tunnel by 'legging' – lying on their backs and

pushing against the tunnel roof. But the roof was too high, so the boatmen had to use poles instead.

At its height in 1789 the canal carried 74,000 tons of goods, mainly coal, and prospered until the railways became established in the 1930s. The section near West Stockwith (*inset*) continued to carry freight until 1955, but the canal was finally abandoned in 1962.

In the years that followed the canal fell into disrepair and might even be an eyesore today but for the efforts of the volunteer teams who have restored sections back to full use.

# North and South Leverton

*I had rather live with cheese and garlic in a windmill far than feed on cakes*
William Shakespeare, *Henry IV Part I*

These villages, five miles east of Retford, and a little over two miles from the River Trent, are two of the many, on both sides of the river, that were settled by Anglo-Saxon tribes in the 5th and 6th centuries onwards.

Today, North Leverton with Habblesthorpe is the official name for the northern village. Habblesthorpe is not mentioned in the Domesday Book but the -thorpe part of its name would indicate that it was settled later, during the period when Danish tribes occupied this part of the county. Now undistinguished from the rest of the village it was formerly of some importance and the site of its vanished church is known.

The establishment of the railway line from Retford to Lincoln effectively divided North and South Leverton physically. While both have the typical warm red brick dwellings prevalent in North Nottinghamshire, South Leverton is particularly rich in such buildings and has good examples of 'tumbling', the method of laying bricks in sloping courses at right angles to the edge of gables (*inset*). There is also a dovecote with stepped gables, and Diamond House, built in 1691 as Sampson's endowed school, continuing as a school until about 40 years ago. The church has a Norman west tower and south porch.

In the 20th century the River Trent, which influenced the early settlers to the Levertons, played a prominent role. This has led to the establishment of two large power stations at West Burton and Cottam. Modern houses have been built at North Leverton to house their workers.

The most interesting building in North Leverton, however, is the windmill (*opposite*) – half a mile west of the village – one of only two working windmills in the county. It is a three-storey building with an ogee cap, four patent sails and a fantail. Built in 1813 by a group of farmers to provide a co-operative means of grinding corn, the mill has worked ever since and now produces grain for animal feeds.

# Hodsock and Worksop Priories

*I dreamed that, as I wandered by the way,*
*Bare winter suddenly was changed to spring*

P.B. Shelley (1792-1822)

While most of Britain's country house gardens are being put to bed for the winter, Hodsock Priory near Blyth is preparing for the arrival in February of thousands of visitors, sometimes from as far afield as America and Japan.

The attraction is Hodsock's beautiful snowdrops (*opposite*), seen carpeting the ground as one walks through lovely woodland. Little known varieties are combined here with common snowdrops to produce one of the most spectacular displays in England.

Hodsock Priory itself, with its imposing medieval red brick gatehouse, never was an actual priory … it was plain Hodsock or Hodsock Hall until the 19th century, and is still a family home. The gardens are in the centre of an 800 acre estate, which is run in an environmentally-friendly way. The latest addition is a working Victorian apiary with beehives resembling Victorian follies.

Further south is the church of Saints Cuthbert and Mary – Worksop Priory (*inset*). This was founded in the early 12th century by William de Lovetot as an Augustinian house and, of course, suffered the same fate as other religious houses in the 16th century, but fortunately the largely Norman nave was retained when many of the adjoining priory buildings were destroyed. The Lady Chapel remained a ruin for four hundred years until restored in the 19th century. A new east end was added in the 20th century, completed in 1974, and is distinguished externally by a thin flèche. The gatehouse to the south of the church is an imposing, mainly 14th century structure.

# Wellow and Ollerton

*Merrily, merrily whirled the wheels of the dizzying dances,*
*Under the orchard-trees and down the path to the meadows.*
Henry Wadsworth Longfellow (1807-1882), *Evangeline*

With its village green, Georgian chapel, red-brick cottages and pantiled roofs alone, Wellow must be considered as the 'beau ideal' of an English village. Add to this its maypole and it can claim perhaps to be the most attractive village in Nottinghamshire.

Wellow long enjoyed the patronage of the Saville family, which also traditionally provided the wooden maypole. A member of the family gave one in 1887 to commemorate Queen Victoria's Golden Jubilee. This pole lasted until 1923 when it was replaced by a new one

as a memorial to men of the village who were killed in the First World War. In the Second World War, ten feet had to be lopped off the top as it was unsafe. The present one is unlikely to suffer the same fate as it is made of steel donated by a local industrialist in 1976. It is 55 feet high and is surmounted by the figure of a cockerel – the tallest permanent maypole in England. The ancient tradition of celebrating the end of winter by dancing round the maypole was revived in 1950. This was usually done on May Day but is now performed at the Spring Bank Holiday (*opposite*).

Just to the north-west of Wellow, Ollerton is almost the central point of Nottinghamshire and owed its existence as a market town to its position near the crossroads of two main highways. The original village still retains much of its earlier character in the area around the church of St Giles, and nearby is the Hop Pole hotel which would have been important as a staging post in the days of coaches. It is a large three-storey building, formerly an 18th century house. The sign reflects the considerable amount of hop growing which took place around Ollerton and Retford in the early 19th century. Opposite is another inn, formerly a smaller late 17th century farmhouse. The River Maun flows through the village and on its way powers a watermill (*inset*) with its wheel still intact. The first floor now houses a teashop which has received awards for its excellence.

# Travelling by Rail

*When a train pulls in to a great city I am reminded of the closing moments of an overture*
Graham Greene (1904-91)

Nottinghamshire is keeping faith with its long history of railway transport. There are projects all around the county to remind us of the great days of steam, to take us into the next century of futuristic travel, and to bring an important, but abandoned route back into use.

The **old** can be found at the Nottingham Transport Heritage Centre (*opposite*) at Rushcliffe Country Park, Ruddington, where on many weekends of the year preserved steam engines are fired up by volunteers to

travel along relaid track to Loughborough. This line, from a former Ministry of Defence depot was once connected to the Great Central mainline.

The **new** comes in the form of Express Transit trams for Nottingham – a futuristic tram system to modernise city commuting. There is some irony in the fact that Nottingham once had a very effective electric tram system which operated between 1901 and 1936 on routes around the city, but it was overtaken by progress and the arrival of the car and motor bus. As the new tram lines were being laid in the city some of the original lines, which had been covered by layers of tarmac, were uncovered.

The **revived** comes in the shape of the Robin Hood Line … the reopening of a railway link between Nottingham, Mansfield (*inset*) and Worksop.

When Dr Beeching's axe fell in the early 1960s, the Nottingham–Worksop passenger service was withdrawn leaving Mansfield as the largest town in Britain without a railway station. But since the beginning of the 1990s, and with the help of European funding, work has led, stage by stage, to the full restoration of a most valuable route, particularly in helping to provide transport for all those affected by the closure of many Nottinghamshire collieries.

# The Rural Landscape

*How blest beyond all blessings are farmers, if they but knew their happiness!*

Virgil

Farming in Nottinghamshire has changed dramatically over the last century – affected by a host of economic factors.

Extensive dairy farming across the county has declined, with the shift being towards more acres of arable crops. And the once high numbers of self-sufficient small farm holdings have given way to farming, over larger areas, of crops such as sugar beet and rape seed by contractors with powerful machinery.

Despite its reputation as a county of coal mining and industry, vast expanses of Nottinghamshire remain as farmland and open countryside. To the south of the county farmland stretches into the peaceful areas of the Vale of Belvoir where the ideal dairy farming conditions have helped create the centre for Britain's Stilton cheese making.

In the north of the county extensive areas of farmland are worked on and around The Dukeries – a region originally comprising great country estates. To the north-west are the remains of Sherwood Forest and modern forestry plantations.

The demise of the mining industry in Nottinghamshire has led to some areas being reclaimed for agriculture, including former spoil tips.

Britain's only surviving example of medieval strip field farming still in operation is at Laxton in the north of the county where, in the Middle Ages, the village was the administration centre of Sherwood Forest. The unenclosed land on several hundred acres is divided into three fields – Mill Field, South Field and West Field – and is currently farmed by 14 tenant farmers in the traditional way. Each tenant is allocated ten strips annually by a 'jury' which aims to ensure fair shares of good and poor land and adjudicates if the rules are broken.

Our pictures are taken at Blue Barn Farm, Nether Langwith in the very north of Nottinghamshire where the village is divided by the county boundary.

**Derek Forss** has over 40 years' experience as a landscape photographer. His work is sponsored by Olympus Cameras and he has contributed to many magazines and books including *Landscapes of Surrey*, where he was responsible for all the photographs. He also lectures to photographic clubs and organises digital photography holidays.

**Mike Astill** from Cotgrave has lived and worked in Nottinghamshire all his life. He began his career as a journalist at the age of 20 reporting for the Newark Advertiser. He has also worked on the Nottingham Evening Post and has been editor of the Trader Group of newspapers and the Herald & Post group. He is currently editor of the county magazine *Nottinghamshire Today*.

*Front cover photograph:* Newark
*Back cover photograph:* Nottingham Goose Fair